Fabulous Sleepovers

Fabulous Sleepovers

by Kris Hirschmann

illustrated by Tom Patrick

Thanks to Deanna for sharing some
of her sleepover secrets.
—*K.H.*

ISBN 0-8167-7441-2

Printed in China.

10 9 8 7 6 5 4 3 2 1

Table of Contents

— Introduction —

So you want to have a sleepover. Great idea! Sleepovers are tons of fun. They strengthen the bonds you already have with your best friends, and they're a super way to get to know new friends better, too.

You'll probably have a blast no matter what you do at your party. But if you want to throw a really *fabulous* sleepover, then you've come to the right place. This book is packed with ideas for movies, food, games, activities, and themes that will help you plan the best sleepover *ever*. Your parents will love these ideas because they don't take a lot of time to prepare or cost tons of money. You and your friends will love them just because you'll have a great time!

As the sleepover hostess, you need to remember one important thing: Great parties don't just happen. They take some planning. But as you will see, the planning process doesn't have to be difficult. In fact, it can be a lot of fun. And keep in mind, a little up-front effort will make your party run smoothly and guarantee that everyone enjoys herself. And that's what a sleepover is all about!

Get Ready!

Preparation is the key to a great sleepover. First, of course, you have to get your parents' permission. Then you need to decide who to invite—and how to invite them, too. (You can get really creative with your party invitations!) Once you've decided how many guests will attend your sleepover, you get to go shopping for food, prizes, videos, and other goodies. (Shopping is a fun part!) And finally, you must decide where and how to set up the actual party room.

None of these preparation steps are hard. But they do take a little time and effort. You should begin planning at least two weeks before the party date so you will have plenty of time to get ready. You could also split up the planning responsibilities with your parents, if they're willing to help. That way no one will have too much to do.

Are you ready to get started? Then keep reading. Let's plan the most fabulous sleepover ever!

GROUND RULES

Talking with your parents is the very first step in planning a sleepover. Tell them what kind of sleepover you want to have—when, how many guests, types of activities, types of food, and any other specifics you have in mind. Once your parents give you permission to have the party, discuss and make decisions about these questions and any others that occur to you:

- What time will the sleepover start, and what time will it end the next day?
- Will there will be a lights-out time? If so, what is it?
- Are there areas of the house that will be off-limits to your guests?
- Is there anything specific you are not allowed to do? (For instance, your parents might not want you to play rowdy games in which you could break things.)
- What kind of privacy will you have? (For instance, are you allowed to close the door to the party room? Does your little brother have to be around?)

CHOOSING YOUR GUESTS

After you have set the ground rules, it's time to

make your guest list. How do you choose? Here are some guidelines.

◻ In general, it's best to invite girls who already know one another and who get along. You can invite new friends if you want to, of course, but you will have to take extra care to make them feel welcome and included.

◻ Don't invite too many people. Most girls say that four or five guests is the perfect number for a sleepover. And one girl had this to say: "My mom taught me that there should always be an even number of people at a sleepover, including myself. That way, if everyone pairs off, no one will be left out."

◻ If you must leave a friend off your list, be kind. Don't talk about your upcoming sleepover in front of her.

IRRESISTIBLE INVITATIONS

Once you have chosen your guests, it's time to create your invitations. You can do something traditional, like calling everyone or giving out pre-printed invites. But why be traditional? Get creative! Here are a few fun ideas to get you started.

◻ **Send e-vites.** E-vites are electronic invitations. You design the card on-line, then input your guests' e-mail addresses. The e-vite then beams straight to their computers! Check out these web sites for free e-vite options: **www.bluemountain.com** and **www.evite.com.** (Ask your parents for permission first, because you have to register.)

☐ **T-shirt fun.** Buy a solid-color pocket T-shirt for each guest. Use a fabric pen to write your invitation information on the pocket. Make sure you tell your guests to bring their T-shirt invitations with them to the party. At your sleepover, provide puff pens, fabric paints, glitter glue, and other materials so each girl can decorate the rest of her T-shirt however she likes. What a great souvenir!

☐ **Picture perfect.** You can mail photographs just like postcards! Choose an appropriate photo, like your house at night or yourself in funny sunglasses, and have a copy made for each guest. Write your invitation information on the back, on the left side. Then address each photo on the right side, stick a stamp in the upper right-hand corner, and drop your picture-perfect invitations into the mail.

You don't have to use these ideas. You can make up your own. Go nuts! The more creative you are, the more excited your guests will be about your fabulous sleepover. But no matter what you do, don't forget to include this important information:

- Your name
- Party location, including address
- Your phone number
- The date of the party
- Time the party starts
- Time the party ends
- Anything special you want your guests to bring

GREAT GIVEAWAYS

No sleepover is complete without giveaways—cool stuff you give to your guests. Giveaways have two purposes. First, they put people in a good mood. (Everyone loves getting free stuff.) But even more important, they can spice up your party. Give your friends things that will keep everyone busy and happy all night long!

Here are some ideas for can't-miss giveaways.

☐ **Goodie bags.** Goodie bags are a sleepover essential! You should provide one goodie bag for each guest. Fill the bags with fun stuff you can use during the party: makeup, hair accessories, nail polish, temporary tattoos, milky pens and black paper, toothbrushes, toiletries, candy, beads, mini flashlights, autograph books, tiny stuffed animals.

☐ **Prizes.** If you will be playing games during your party, consider giving out inexpensive prizes to the winners. Make sure you get enough for everyone so no one will feel left out. You could even get some consolation prizes for girls who don't win any games.

☐**Craft basics.** Give everyone something she can decorate during the night: a baseball cap, a pair of socks, or anything else you like. Individual bead animal kits or other cool crafts are lots of fun, too!

GO SHOPPING

A day or two before your sleepover, plan a big shopping trip to get all the supplies you need. Use the Essential Sleepover Supplies checklist on page 17 to help you plan your trip. You won't need to buy everything on the list—you can find many supplies around your home—but some things, like food and prizes, will probably need to be purchased especially for your party.

And don't forget to rent plenty of movies! Check out the Must-See Movies list on page 16 if you need ideas.

SET UP YOUR SPACE

On the day of your sleepover, set up a special party area. Here are a few things to keep in mind.

☐**Move all breakable objects** away from the party zone. No matter how careful you and your guests are, accidents can happen if things are in the way.

☐**Decorate, decorate, decorate.** Decorations like balloons and streamers give your sleepover space that little extra something! You could also hang strings of twinkling lights around the room, put up posters, or do anything else you'd like to create a festive atmosphere.

☐ **Make sure everything works.** Test the CD player, the VCR, the television, remote controls, and any other electronics you plan to use during your party.

☐ **Consider the comfort factor.** Are there plenty of places for your guests to lounge? If not, you might want to make a mountain of throw pillows in the middle of the floor. Or you could blow up a couple of air mattresses. Even plastic floats will do!

☐ **Gather everything you need.** You don't want to bother looking for games, CDs, paper, craft supplies, and other essentials during your sleepover. Collect everything in a big box and stick it in a corner of the party room.

☐ **Prepare for your activities.** Do you need a table for crafts? A stage area for karaoke? Computer access for on-line fun? Think about the things you will need for your planned activities, and make sure all those things are set up before your guests arrive.

☐ **Arrange a separate sleepy area.** Some of your guests may not want to stay up as late as others. Be considerate and set up a quiet early-to-bed area for sleepyheads.

TIME TO PARTY!

Once you have accomplished everything in this chapter, it's time to party. All you need now are your guests!

❄ Must-See Movies ❄

Classic Comedies:
Babe
Big
Bring It On*
Dr. Dolittle*
George of the Jungle
Home Alone
Hook
A League of Their Own
The Mighty Ducks
The Princess Diaries

Rockin' Romances:
10 Things I Hate About You*
Ever After
Ghost*
Grease
Never Been Kissed*
The Princess Bride
Save the Last Dance*
Sleepless in Seattle
The Wedding Planner*
While You Were Sleeping

Cool Cartoons:
A Bug's Life
Charlotte's Web
Mulan
101 Dalmatians
Shrek
Toy Story I & II
Who Framed Roger Rabbit?

Scary Stuff:
Beetlejuice
Buffy the Vampire Slayer*
Dracula (the old one)
Frankenstein (the old one)
The Mummy*
Poltergeist
The Sixth Sense*

*These movies are rated PG-13. Ask a parent for permission.

Checklist:
✿ Essential Sleepover Supplies ✿

Night-lights ____
(so your guests can find the bathroom and the kitchen when it gets dark)

Flashlights ____
(one for each guest)

**Extra batteries
for flashlights** ____

Clock or watch ____
(you want to see how LATE it's getting!)

Camera and film ____

Munchies ____

Drinks ____

**"Real meal" food,
including dinner
and breakfast** ____

**Disposable plates,
cups, napkins,
utensils** ____

Garbage can ____
(it's best to have one in your party room)

Guest goodie bags ____

Prizes ____

CD or tape player ____

CDs or tapes ____

Movies ____

Craft materials ____
(see the "Cool Crafts" section for ideas)

**Plenty of paper
and pencils** ____

Fun magazines ____

Board games ____

Stopwatch ____
(just in case you want to time something)

Pillows ____
(make a big pile so your guests can lounge in comfort!)

Blankets ____
(for warmth when watching videos)

Decorations ____

**Plastic laundry bag
for each guest** ____

**Towel and washcloth
for each guest** ____

2

Fun Food

Let's be honest. A sleepover just wouldn't be a sleepover if you and your friends didn't gorge yourselves on tasty junk foods like pizza, hot dogs, candy, and soda. In fact, the food is a big part of the fun—and as the party hostess, you are the Munchie Queen! It's up to you to make sure your guests are well-fed and happy.

Planning the food for your sleepover is a big job. You have to decide what meals you want to serve, what munchies to have on hand, and how much of everything to buy. You also have to make sure there is something for everyone. Yikes! It can be confusing. But luckily, your parents are GREAT at planning meals and grocery shopping. They do it all the time. So don't hesitate to ask them for help. It will make your life a lot easier.

There's another reason to get your parents involved, too. You might need a grown-up to help you with food that has to be cooked, baked, blended, or microwaved. So it's best if everyone agrees on the party menu up front.

PLANNING YOUR MENU

So how exactly *do* you start planning your menu? There are a few things to keep in mind.

- **Don't forget a meal!** You're going to be serving two full meals: dinner and breakfast. Plan menus for both. (See Chapter 9, "Good Morning!" for breakfast ideas and recipes.) You'll also need plenty of snacks that people can munch on in between meals, and lots of drinks, too. It's going to be a loo*oooong* night, and your guests will want to nibble!

- **Provide something for everyone.** (Use the Get the Munchies checklist on page 29 if you need ideas.) Some girls like salty snacks; some have a sweet tooth. Some girls might be vegetarians or have other special dietary needs. Some might like only healthy snacks. Remember, it's perfectly okay to ask your guests what they like if you're not sure. Just do it *before* the party so you'll be able to add their suggestions to your grocery list.

☐ **Buy a little extra.** Any hostess will tell you that it's better to have too much food than too little. Don't worry, nothing will go to waste. Your family can eat the leftovers after the party ends.

MAKE MEALTIME AN EVENT

There's nothing wrong with serving a regular sit-down meal to your guests. Pizza, hot dogs, and burgers are *always* popular. With a little advance planning, however, you can let your guests create their own meals. Doing this is fun, it's yummy, and it turns each meal into an event!

There are several recipes at the end of this chapter for make-your-own meals and snacks. Try them out, or come up with an original idea. (Hey! Wouldn't that be *make-up-your-own make-your-own food?*)

DURING THE PARTY

All of your careful food planning leads up to the main event: your sleepover. At the party, you can take care of your guests by following these simple steps.

☐ **Know your food responsibilities.** Before your sleepover, decide who will handle the food duties. If a parent is willing to help you out, that's great. He or she can make sure the meals get served on time. The parent can also keep chip bowls full, sodas on ice, and

popcorn popping. But if these jobs will be up to you, make sure you take them seriously! A good hostess never lets her guests go hungry or thirsty, not even for a moment.

☐ **Give your guests a food tour.** After your guests arrive, show them where the food is. Ask them to let you or your parents know right away if something runs out so it can be refilled.

☐ **Tell your guests the "food rules."** Do you expect each girl to help herself, or should she ask whenever she wants another soda or snack? Are there certain areas where eating and drinking are not allowed? Are your guests allowed to use the microwave oven, the toaster, and other appliances? Make sure everyone understands these and any other food rules.

That's really all you need to know. The most important thing is just to make sure there are plenty of munchies to go around. Full bellies mean happy guests!

GREAT RECIPES

The next few pages contain some tasty, time-tested recipes. Some require group participation; others can be done in advance. Pick the ones that suit your party style and your taste buds, and let's get cooking!

Top-Your-Own Mini Pizzas

Basic ingredients:
- English muffin halves or sandwich-size loaves of French bread, cut in half
- Pizza sauce
- Shredded mozzarella cheese

Toppings (set out in dishes with serving utensils):

• Pepperoni slices	• Ham chunks
• Onion slivers	• Chopped tomato chunks
• Cooked sausage pieces	• Green pepper slices
• Sliced mushrooms	• Anything else you like

Each girl puts pizza sauce on an English muffin or French bread half, then sprinkles plenty of mozzarella cheese on top. Now comes the fun part! Each girl gets to choose her own toppings and design her own custom pizza. When everyone is done, have an adult bake the pizzas in the oven at 350 degrees Fahrenheit (about 175 degrees Celsius) for 10 to 15 minutes, or until the cheese is hot and bubbly. Serve and enjoy!

Itsy Bitsy Sandwich Bites

Basic ingredients:
- Any kind of small bread (mini bagels, dinner rolls, or rye rounds are perfect)

Fillings (set out in dishes with serving utensils):
- Tuna salad
- Chicken salad
- Peanut butter
- Jelly
- Cheese
- Assorted lunch meats
- Anything else you like

Toppings and condiments:
- Lettuce
- Tomatoes
- Pickles
- Mayonnaise
- Mustard
- Anything else you like

Set all the ingredients on a table, then let your guests go wild making whatever kinds of sandwiches they like. This is fun because everyone gets exactly what she wants. And because these sandwiches are so tiny, your guests can make several and get a little taste of everything!

Fill-Them-Yourself Pigs in Blankets

Basic ingredients:
- Hot dogs
- Refrigerated crescent roll dough

Fillings (set out in dishes with serving utensils):
- Grated cheese
- Minced onions
- Ketchup
- Sauerkraut
- Mustard
- Hot dog relish

Each girl lays a hot dog across a piece of crescent roll dough. She adds whatever fillings she likes, then rolls everything up. (Make sure to pinch the dough closed.) Place each pig on a cookie sheet—remember which pig belongs to each girl! Have an adult bake the finished pigs in blankets according to the directions on the crescent roll package. When the piggies are cooked, remove them from the oven and pig out!

Did You Know? April 24 is National Pigs in a Blanket Day.

Easy Popcorn Balls

Ingredients:
- 1/2 cup (120 ml) honey
- 1/4 cup (60 ml) sugar
- 1/2 tsp. (2.5 ml) ground cinnamon
- Butter
- 1 bag **plain** popped microwave popcorn

Combine the honey, the sugar, the cinnamon, and 1 tablespoon (15 ml) of butter in a large microwave-safe bowl. Cover the bowl with plastic wrap, then have an adult microwave the mixture at high power for 2 1/2 to 3 minutes. Remove the bowl from the microwave and add the popcorn. Stir with a wooden spoon until all of the popcorn is coated with the honey/sugar goop. Let everything sit for a few minutes or until it is cool enough to handle. Smear butter all over your palms, grab a handful of the popcorn mixture, and shape it into a ball. Repeat until all of the mixture has been made into tasty popcorn balls.

The balls will be soft at first, but they will get harder after they sit and cool for a while.

No-Cook Mini S'Mores

Ingredients:
• Graham crackers
• Marshmallow Fluff
• Hershey's chocolate bars

Break a whole graham cracker into four even rectangles. (Most graham crackers have perforations baked right into them that show you where to break.) Smear one side each of two rectangles with Marshmallow Fluff. Sandwich the two crackers, Fluff side in, around two squares of chocolate from a Hershey's bar. Ta-da! Instant s'mores!

Invent-Your-Own Ice Cream Delights

There's no right or wrong way to do this one. Just set out lots of yummy ice creams and toppings and let each guest create her own ice cream delight! You can provide any ingredients you like, but here are some suggestions to get you started.

• Ice cream (of course!)
• Sauces: chocolate, hot fudge, caramel, butterscotch, strawberry

- Fruit: bananas, cherries, sliced strawberries, blueberries, crushed pineapple
- Toppings: chopped nuts, chocolate and multi-colored sprinkles, mini chocolate chips, Oreo cookie crumbs, M&M's
- Whipped cream or Cool Whip

Scrumptious Fruit Smoothies

There are so many great smoothie recipes that it's hard to know where to start! Try these favorites, or make up your own. (Be sure to get a parent's help. You need a blender to make smoothies.)

Some of these recipes call for frozen yogurt. This does not mean the ice cream kind. It means regular yogurt that has been chilled in the freezer for a few hours.

- **Strawberry Smoothie:** Blend five large strawberries, 6 ounces (180 ml) of frozen strawberry yogurt, and 4 ounces (120 ml) of lemonade.
- **Chocolate-Banana Smoothie:** Blend one sliced banana, 1/4 cup (60 ml) of milk, 6 ounces (180 ml) of chocolate yogurt (not frozen), and three large ice cubes.
- **Melon Ball Smoothie:** Blend 2/3 cup (160 ml) of chopped cantaloupe, 2/3 cup (160 ml) of chopped honeydew, 8 ounces (240 ml) of frozen peach yogurt, 1 cup (240 ml) of milk, and four ice cubes.

- **Tropical Smoothie:** Blend one banana, 6 ounces (180 ml) of frozen peach yogurt, and 6 ounces (180 ml) of pineapple-orange-banana juice.
- **Piña Colada Smoothie:** Blend 1/2 frozen banana, 6 ounces (180 ml) of frozen coconut yogurt, 10 ounces (300 ml) of crushed pineapple, and 8 ounces (240 ml) of milk.

If your smoothie is too runny, add more fruit or a couple of ice cubes. If your smoothie is too thick, add some more milk or juice, whichever your recipe calls for.

Checklist:
❄ Get the Munchies ❄

Do you need munchie ideas for your sleepover? Here are some all-time favorite snacks and drinks. Check off the ones that are essential to *your* party!

Salty stuff:
Popcorn ____
Potato chips ____
Nuts ____
Crackers ____
Pretzels ____

Sweet stuff:
Cookies ____
Marshmallows ____
Cake ____
Popsicles ____

Candy:
Mini candy bars ____
M&M's ____
Red Hots ____
Tootsie Rolls ____
Your favorite ____

Healthy stuff:
Cut-up veggies ____
Veggie dip ____
Fruit salad ____
Plain raisins ____
Yogurt raisins ____
Granola bars ____

Drinks:
Soda ____
Juice ____
Bottled water ____
Regular milk ____
Flavored milk ____
Iced tea ____
Hot chocolate ____

Other things I need:

_____
_____
_____
_____

Quiz:
❄ Junk Food Junkie? ❄

How much do you and your friends know about junk food? Take this quick nutrition quiz to find out.

1. Which drink does not contain caffeine?
A. Diet Coke   B. Hot chocolate   C. Milk   D. Iced tea

2. Which snack is fat free?
A. Red Hots   B. Milk   C. Crackers   D. Granola

3. Which snack contains the most fat?
A. Celery   B. Granola   C. Iced tea   D. Tootsie Rolls

4. Which snack has the most calories?
A. 20 mini marshmallows   C. 10 baby carrots
B. Small can of apple juice   D. Popsicle

5. Which snack has the least calories?
A. Handful of M&M's   C. Handful of raisins
B. Can of regular soda   D. 3 cups microwave popcorn

6. Which snack is sugar free?
A. Water   B. Tootsie Rolls   C. Crackers   D. Granola

7. Which snack contains protein?
A. Potato chips   B. Cake   C. Nuts   D. Fruit

8. How many calories in a pound/kilo?
A. 2500/5500   C. 3500/7700
B. 3000/6600   D. 4000/8800

Answers: 1C, 2A, 3B, 4B, 5D, 6A, 7C, 8C

30

Great Games

It's hard to beat that feeling you get from laughing with your friends. If you want lots of laughs at your sleepover, then you should plan some goofy games and activities. Why? Playing games is a super way to give your guests the giggles. Games are also good for increasing the energy level of your sleepover and ensuring that everyone has a great time!

You probably have plenty of ideas of your own—but if you need some help, this chapter contains eleven games that are guaranteed to pump up the fun factor. All of these games can be played by any number of people. You can follow the rules in the book or change them to suit your sleepover personality. It's completely up to you!

GAME BASICS

Although there are no hard-and-fast rules about

which games to play at your party, there are a few guidelines to follow.

☐ **Choose games beforehand.** Think about what games you would like to play well before the party date. This will give you time to prepare and also to select prizes, if necessary. Some fun activities (such as Musical Gift on page 33 and Scavenger Hunt on page 36) require advance planning.

☐ **Choose games that everyone will enjoy.** If you know that one of your friends hates Monopoly, for example, you probably shouldn't plan a Monopoly tournament.

☐ **Plan around your friends' personalities.** If you and your friends are outgoing, then activities like karaoke might be perfect for your sleepover. But shy guests might not enjoy this type of game. Also, you don't want to play anything that might hurt someone's feelings. Some of your friends might love playing Truth or Dare, for example, but others might get embarrassed and upset. Nothing ruins a party faster than arguments and angry feelings, so avoid activities that could be "hot spots." Only you know what these hot spots are; every group is different.

☐ **Plan a variety of games.** Pick some games that are lively and loud. (Musical Sleeping Bags on page 34 is a good example.) Also pick some that are quiet and thoughtful. (Your Secret Self on page 35 is a good example.) Play the more energetic games early on, when everyone is still wide awake and excited. Play quieter games later, when everyone has calmed down a little (and other family members may be trying to sleep).

☐ **Everybody must be able to play at once.** It's not much fun watching two people play Nintendo for hours. Choose activities in which everyone can participate.

Remember, choosing games is about common sense and personal preference. Pick several activities that sound like fun to you, then get ready to have a great time!

MUSICAL GIFT

To prepare for this game, wrap a small prize in a small box. Put the small wrapped box into a slightly larger box and wrap it up again. Repeat until the prize is buried inside as many boxes as possible. Ten or even more is good, if you can find that many containers.

To play the game, everyone sits in a circle. Ask an adult helper to play some music in the background. While the music is going, players pass the box around the circle from one girl to the next. When the music stops, the girl holding the box gets to unwrap the top layer. Then the music resumes and players begin passing the box again. The girl who unwraps the final layer gets to keep the prize.

MUSICAL SLEEPING BAGS

Arrange your sleeping bags in a star-burst shape on the floor with the open ends pointing out. There should be one less sleeping bag than players.

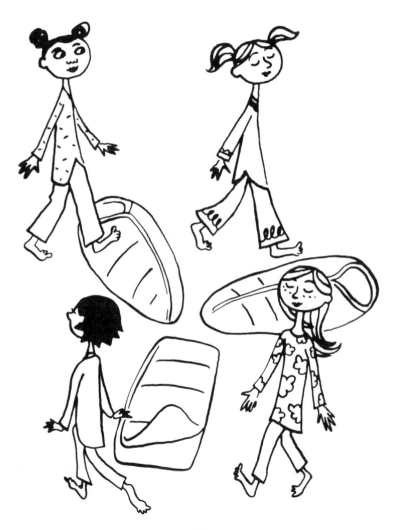

An adult helper plays music. While the music is going, players walk around the sleeping bag circle. When the music stops, each player tries to scramble into a sleeping bag. The girl who doesn't get a sleeping bag is out of the game. The other players remove one sleeping bag, the music resumes, and everyone walks until the music stops again. Then there is another scramble.

This is repeated until only one player is left in the game. Crown her the winner!

TOUCHY FEELY

This is another fun sleeping bag game. Choose one girl to be "It." Have her leave the room, then let another girl hide inside a sleeping bag. Make sure no part of the hiding girl shows. Then everyone else hides under a blanket. The girl who is "It" comes back into the room and tries to figure out who is in the sleeping bag by touch alone. Be quiet—if you're the "hider," your giggles may give you away!

YOUR SECRET SELF

Have each girl answer the questions on the Your Secret Self questionnaire on page 42. (Make a photocopy of the questionnaire for each girl if possible.) Choose one person to read the completed sheets out loud. Then everyone tries to guess who filled out each questionnaire. How well do you really know your friends? You're about to find out!

SCAVENGER HUNT

This party classic never goes out of style! It does take a little advance preparation, though, so be sure to set this activity up before the party begins.

To prepare the scavenger hunt, carefully look around your party room and make a list of things to find. (Ask a parent to do this for you if you want to enjoy the hunting fun along with your friends.) Your items can be easy and obvious, like "lamp" or "pillow." Or they can be harder, like "a three-letter word" (think magazine covers and book spines) or "something that starts with T." Make sure you put a few hard-to-find items on your list, or else the game will be over too quickly.

When you are ready to begin the hunt, give each guest a list and a pencil and shout "Go!" Each girl should try to check off everything on the list. The first one to succeed wins the game!

SING-ALONG FUN

It doesn't matter whether you're a great singer or a lousy one. Karaoke (singing along with your favorite songs) is fun to perform and even more fun to watch!

For a professional presentation, set up a small stage at one end of your party space where each performer can strut her stuff. You can buy special karaoke music if you want. Most music stores carry recordings of popular music without the vocal tracks. These recordings are ideal for sing-along fun. Of course, you can always just belt out the tunes right along with the performers on your favorite CDs or tapes, too.

There are even some web sites for karaoke, with lyrics and everything! A couple of good ones are **www.thinks.com/karaoke** and **www.bored.com/ karaoke/pop.htm.**

TRUTH OR DARE

Truth or Dare may be the best sleepover game ever invented. You get to learn your friends' deep, dark secrets, and you get to be active and silly, too. Could there be a better combination than that?

The game is simple. Get a bunch of small slips of paper. On one side of each slip, write a "truth" challenge. On the other side, write a "dare" challenge. (There are some ideas to get you started on page 43.) Drop all the slips into a box.

Now take turns asking each girl, "Truth or dare?" The girl must say whether she wants to answer a truth question or perform a dare. After she makes her choice, draw a slip from the box and read the chosen challenge. If it's a "truth," the girl must answer honestly. If it's a "dare," she has to do whatever the paper says, no matter how goofy or embarrassing!

Here's a warning! Although Truth or Dare is lots of fun, it can sometimes get out of hand. You and your friends may be sharing some very personal things, so you must be careful not to upset anyone. To avoid hurt feelings, many girls like to have a "Pass" rule when they play Truth or Dare. In this version of the game, each player gets to "pass" on two challenges without penalty. Any player who refuses a third challenge is out of the game. The boldest players will last the longest . . . and one brave girl will eventually emerge as the winner!

COMEDY CONTEST

Here's your chance to be a stand-up comedienne. Everybody takes turns telling the funniest jokes she knows. You can just do this for fun, or you can make it into a real contest. Here's how: If no one laughs at a girl's joke (or if she can't think of a joke to tell), then that girl is out. The girl who stays in the contest the longest is the comedy champion!

If you want to make the most of your comedy competition, tell your guests about it in advance. You could even mention it on the sleepover invitation. The jokes will probably be a lot better if everyone has some time to prepare.

JOKE CIRCLE

Here's another fun joke-related activity. Have all your guests lie in a circle on the floor. Each girl should lay her head on another girl's stomach.

Now take turns telling jokes or making funny comments. The goal of the game is to avoid laughing. But before long, someone is guaranteed to giggle—and when this happens, watch out! The giggling girl's stomach will bounce. This will make the girl whose head is lying on the giggler's stomach laugh, too. The laughter will spread around the circle as more and more girls lose control, and pretty soon you'll be bouncing all over!

TELEPHONE

The game of Telephone is an old sleepover favorite, and with good reason. The results can be side-splitting!

To play Telephone, have all your guests sit in a circle. One girl thinks of a phrase, then whispers it into the next girl's ear. That girl then whispers the phrase into the next girl's ear, and so on. The last girl says the phrase out loud. You'd think the phrase would be the same as it was in the beginning, but it almost never is! The phrase usually changes a lot between the first girl and the last girl, and the changes make for a lot of laughs.

There's just one important rule to remember when playing Telephone: *The whisperer never, ever repeats a phrase.* If the listening girl doesn't quite hear everything, too bad! She has to do the best she can to figure out what the whisperer said without any additional hints. Why? Well, if everyone could hear perfectly all the time, the results wouldn't be nearly as funny!

FILL-IN-THE-BLANK FORTUNES

This activity is not only funny, it also lets you take a peek into your "future." (Okay, so maybe you can't *really* see the future. But it's fun to pretend!)

To come up with the "fortunes," ask each guest to write down a list of words that fit the categories on page 44. For example, a girl could write "France" for No. 1, "the Great Pyramids" for No. 2, "bugs" for No. 3, "rocks" for No. 4, and so on. Do not let anyone look at the fortune before writing down her words!

When all the lists are done, have each girl read "Your Future" on page 45 out loud, inserting her words into the blanks as she goes. If you used the words from the example above, this is what the first sentence would say: "You will travel to France, where you will see the Great Pyramids and learn to love strange native foods like bugs and rocks." Pretty goofy, eh?

The great thing about this activity is that everyone's fortune will be different, but they will *all* be good for a laugh!

Questionnaire:
❈ Your Secret Self ❈

Everyone at your sleepover, including you, should answer these questions. Read the answer sheets out loud and see if you can guess the authors!

Name your favorite:

Food _____   Movie or TV star _____

Drink _____   Singer or group _____

Color _____   Holiday _____

TV show _____   Store _____

Song _____   School subject _____

Sport _____   Magazine _____

What is your zodiac sign? _____

What is your middle name? _____

If you could be any animal, what would you be and why?

_____

_____

What do you want to be when you are older? _____

_____

Name one thing you would change about yourself.

_____

What do you think is your best physical feature?

_____

What makes you a great friend?

_____

Name one thing you are really, really good at doing.

_____

❊ Truth or Dare ❊

Here are some sample Truth or Dare questions and challenges. Use them in your game, make up your own, or do both!

Truth:
- What's the worst name anyone ever called you?
- Describe your most embarrassing moment.
- Tell everyone what your last diary entry was about.
- Reveal something no one knows about you.
- Describe a time your parents embarrassed you in public.
- Describe any dream you've had recently.
- What do you want more than anything else?
- Do you have a secret crush on someone? Who?
- Which teacher do you think is the cutest?
- Name something you're afraid of.
- Name something you really like about yourself.
- Describe the person you would like to marry someday.
- Do you believe in ghosts? Why or why not?

Dare:
- Sing "Happy Birthday" while hopping on one foot.
- Do a funky disco dance while everyone watches.
- Send an e-mail to a boy you like.
- Pretend you're picking your nose.
- Act like a chicken for one minute.
- Do your best impression of any cartoon character.
- Do the hokey pokey. Don't forget to sing the song.
- Eat something slowly while everyone watches. Chew with your mouth open.
- Snort like a pig.
- Impersonate one of your teachers.
- Drink half a can of soda very quickly through a straw.
- Open a magazine to any page. Read something to your friends in your best "actress" voice. Make it dramatic!
- Get down on one knee and propose marriage to someone.

❄ Fill-in-the-Blank Fortunes ❄

Read the instructions on page 41 to find out how to play this game. See what silliness the future holds for you!

1. Foreign country
2. Landmark
3. Something you don't want to eat
4. Another thing you don't want to eat
5. Language
6. Profession
7. Feeling verb (*e.g.*, like, hate)
8. Adjective
9. Animal, plural (*e.g.*, dogs)
10. Animal, plural
11. Adjective
12. Noun
13. Noun
14. Profession
15. Man's name
16. Color
17. Color
18. Height (*e.g.*, 3 feet, 90 inches, 12 meters)
19. Hobby
20. Will or will not (pick one)
21. Type of music
22. Number
23. Color
24. Number
25. Number
26. Adjective
27. Number
28. Adjective
29. Animal
30. Name
31. City
32. Adjective
33. Profession
34. Amount of money
35. Something you wear
36. "ing" verb (*e.g.*, sewing)
37. Name
38. Name
39. Good personality trait
40. Bad personality trait
41. Good personality trait
42. Bad personality trait
43. Adjective
44. Place
45. Will or will not (pick one)

❧ Your Future ❧

Travel

You will travel to ___(1)___, where you will see the ___(2)___ and learn to love strange native foods like ___(3)___ and ___(4)___. You will learn to speak ___(5)___ and will become internationally famous for your skills as a(n) ___(6)___. Everyone will ___(7)___ you! During your travels, you will see many ___(8)___ ___(9)___ and ___(10)___. You will also find a(n) ___(11)___ ___(12)___ in a dark ___(13)___.

Marriage and Family

You will marry a(n) ___(14)___ named ___(15)___. He will have ___(16)___ eyes and ___(17)___ hair, and will be ___(18)___ tall. His favorite hobby will be ___(19)___. He ___(20)___ be a sports nut. His favorite type of music will be ___(21)___. There will be ___(22)___ people at your wedding, and you will wear a(n) ___(23)___ dress. You will be married for ___(24)___ years and will have ___(25)___ ___(26)___ girls and ___(27)___ ___(28)___ boys. You will have a pet ___(29)___ named ___(30)___ and you will live in ___(31)___.

Profession

You will become a(n) ___(32)___ ___(33)___. You will make ___(34)___ per year. You will wear ___(35)___ to work and will spend your days ___(36)___. You will work with people named ___(37)___ and ___(38)___. ___(37)___ will be ___(39)___ but ___(40)___, and ___(38)___ will be ___(41)___ but ___(42)___. You will work in a(n) ___(43)___ ___(44)___ and ___(45)___ become famous!

Beauty Basics

Sleepovers provide the perfect opportunity to experiment with makeup, new hairdos, and other beauty basics. You and your guests are going to be together all night long, so you have plenty of time; it's not like you're rushing to get ready for a specific event. And you're not going anywhere, so you can try wild and crazy styles that you might be nervous to wear out into the real world. It doesn't matter whether the results are dumpy or dazzling. After all, it's just us girls!

This chapter includes some tips and ideas for the "big four" of beauty: nail care, skin care, makeup, and hair care. Decide in advance what you would like to do, because all of these activities require special supplies. You will need to prepare. But the glamorous results will make it all worthwhile!

BASIC BEAUTY TIPS

These suggestions will help you make the most of your beauty activities.

☐ **What's your beauty personality?** Copy the quiz on page 57 for each of your guests. When each girl has answered all the questions, compare beauty personalities to figure out which beauty activities suit your group best.

☐ **Share supplies.** Beauty products can be expensive. You probably don't want to buy everything you will need for your party (although you might consider slipping a few cool beauty items into each girl's goodie bag). You also don't want all of your personal everyday supplies to get used up. So ask your guests to bring their favorite beauty products with them. That way, everybody can share.

☐ **But don't share eye makeup.** It's not sanitary. You can spread infections by sharing mascara, eyeliner, and other makeup that goes near the eyes.

☐ **Stock up on magazines.** Before your party, gather a stack of new and old beauty magazines and put them in your party room. When beauty time arrives, you and your guests can use the pictures in the magazines for inspiration.

☐ **Provide old T-shirts.** If you and your guests will be doing something messy, like giving each other facials or putting on glitter gel, then provide an old T-shirt for each girl to wear so she doesn't mess up her good clothes.

☐ **Get permission.** Ask a parent for permission if you're planning to use any electrical beauty appliances (hair dryer, curling iron, hot rollers, etc.).

☐ **Don't forget cleanup supplies.** Some of your guests might not want to "stay beautiful" all night long. Make sure you have cold cream, soap, nail polish remover, and other supplies on hand for guests who want to scrub themselves clean after your beauty session. Some girls might even want to take a shower, so make sure there are enough clean towels to go around. A good hostess prepares for any situation!

Got the ground rules? Great. Let's get gorgeous!

NIFTY NAILS

Having your nails done by someone else is one of the most relaxing beauty experiences there is. You and your guests can follow these easy steps to give one another manicures (on the fingernails) and pedicures (on the toenails).

1. Remove old nail polish using a cotton ball soaked in polish remover.

2. File the nails into shape. There are two main fingernail shapes: square with rounded corners, and oval. Toenails should be filed until they are smooth and nicely rounded.

3. Rub cuticle cream or moisturizing lotion onto the base of each nail, where the skin is.

4. Have the girl soak her hands or feet in warm, soapy water for five minutes.

5. Have the girl remove her hands or feet from the water and dry them off. Use a wooden nail care stick to *gently* push each cuticle back. Be careful!

6. Apply a clear base coat to each nail. Let the nails dry for about five minutes.

7. Apply a coat of colored polish to each nail. Let the nails dry for five minutes, then apply a second coat of the same color.

8. Apply a clear top coat to each nail.

9. Use a cotton swab dipped in polish remover to clean up any polish mistakes you made.

10. Your "client" should be careful about touching anything until her nails are completely dry. This might take some time if you're using regular nail polish. It will be much quicker if you use the fast-drying kind. Any drugstore carries this special nail polish, which works great and is just as pretty as the regular kind.

That's all there is to it! You now know how to give your friends professional-looking manicures and pedicures.

FUN FACIALS

There's nothing like a good facial to make your face squeaky clean and smooth! Home facials are easy, and fun, too. Just follow these simple steps.

1. Start with a facial scrub. There are lots of commercial products you can buy and try. You could also make your own scrub. One beauty contestant recommends a thick mixture of regular oatmeal and plain yogurt. (It sounds funny, but it really works!) Gently massage the scrub into your face for a few minutes to remove dead skin and give you a healthy glow. Rinse your face thoroughly when you're done scrubbing.

2. Steam those pores open! Fill a sink with steaming hot water. Then bend over the sink until your face is just above the water (be careful not to touch the water with your face or hands). Drape a bath towel over your head and the sink so that the steam is trapped inside. Hang out for a few minutes, letting the warm steam bathe your face.

3. Once your skin is nice and sweaty, splash your face several times with lukewarm water. This will clean the dirt out of your pores. (Everyone has dirty stuff in her skin. Don't be embarrassed!)

4. Splash your face several times with cool water to close your pores again. Dry yourself off.

5. Clean your face with an astringent to remove any last bits of oil or dirt.

6. Apply a facial moisturizer.

7. And now for the crowning touch! Lie on your back and close your eyes. Have a friend place a cucumber slice over each eye. Then relax for ten minutes. The cucumbers will suck any puffiness away from your eyelids and leave you looking and feeling your beautiful best!

If you want to get even more ambitious, you could apply a facial mask after your steam treatment. Drugstores carry dozens of brands, and some of them are very reasonably priced.

MARVELOUS MAKEUP

Chances are good that you already know about the different kinds of makeup and how to apply them. So instead of specific makeup instructions, here are some general tips.

☐ Don't try to use makeup to "paint your face" or turn yourself into someone you're not. The main purpose of makeup is to make your good features stand out and to minimize your weak features. Decide which areas you want to emphasize and which ones you want to hide, then pick the right makeup for the job.

☐ On the other hand, a sleepover is the perfect time to be daring and try new makeup products and techniques! Make a pact of total honesty with your friends. Promise you will tell one another which products and techniques look great and which ones make you look like clowns. The next time you apply makeup on your own, you'll remember what worked and what didn't.

☐ Instead of applying your makeup yourself, consider letting a friend do it. Sit quietly with your eyes closed while a buddy plays makeup artist. The fun part comes when she finishes her work and you open your eyes. Surprise! It's a whole new you!

☐ Every girl knows this, but it's so important that it's worth repeating: *Never, ever go to sleep with makeup still on your face.* Makeup clogs your pores, which can lead to acne—and nobody wants that! So wash your face thoroughly with a facial cleanser before you settle down to snooze.

GET WILD!

You don't have to restrict yourself to regular makeup. Experiment with fun stuff like temporary tattoos, glitter gel, and body stickers. You could even buy a commercial *mehndi* (body henna painting) kit if you want to get extra creative.

HAIR CARE

If you've ever dreamed of having movie-star hair, now's your chance. You and your friends can have fun creating the most glamorous and wackiest hairstyles ever!

Before you begin, make sure you have a good supply of essential hair items. This short list will get you started.

- ☐ **The "hardware":** Brushes, combs, hair picks, bobby pins, butterfly clips, elastic bands, hair appliances (blow dryer, curling iron, etc.)
- ☐ **Hairstyle products:** Hair spray, hair gel, mousse, hair glitter, spray-on hair color
- ☐ **Decorations:** Scrunchies, barrettes, hair ties, hair bands, bows, ribbons, beads, clip-on hair charms

Grab whatever items you like and get to work! Encourage everyone to get creative. You won't be going out in public with these funky 'dos.

If you need some ideas, here are a few time-tested techniques you could try.

- ☐ **For body:** Apply mousse to wet hair. Stand bent over with your head down so your hair falls toward the floor. Blow dry your hair most of the way. When it is just a little bit damp, stand up and complete your styling.
- ☐ **Teasing:** Grab a thick lock of hair and hold it straight out from your head. Brush along the lock toward your scalp. Repeat all over your head until your hair stands up in a wild, tangled mane!
- ☐ **For messy curls:** Apply gel to almost-dry hair. Grab a handful of your hair and scrunch it into a ball. Repeat all over your head until your hair is dry. Use a hair pick to shape your curly 'do.

○ **For tiny waves:** Plait dozens of thin braids into your wet hair. Let your hair dry, then undo the braids to release the waves. Shape with a hair pick.

FASHION SHOW

Once everyone is fully beautified, why not put on a fashion show so each girl can strut her stuff? Lay a long piece of fabric on the floor to serve as a "catwalk." Blast the type of energetic pop music you would hear at a real fashion show. Then let each girl take turns walking the catwalk in her best supermodel style.

Of course, you can't have a fashion show without a high-fashion photographer. Get a camera and ask your guests if anyone will volunteer to be the photographer. It will be this girl's job to take pictures of your fashion extravaganza. (Or, if none of your guests would be too embarrassed, perhaps a parent would be willing to take the photos.) After the sleepover, get the pictures developed and give each guest a good shot of herself. The pictures will be great reminders of your fabulous night of beauty!

INNER BEAUTY

Taking care of your outer beauty is fun, and it's something every girl should do. But it is just as important to take care of your inner beauty. There is a saying: "Beauty is only skin deep." This means that no matter how good you look on the outside, it's the inner you that counts the most. Inner beauty has to do with things like confidence, a caring attitude, and a happy nature—which are just the kinds of things you love about your pals!

What is your inner beauty factor? Take the quiz on page 58 to find out. You can keep the results secret or share them with your friends. Either way is fine.

Whatever you score, you should keep one thing in mind. You're taking this quiz at a great sleepover party with a bunch of your buddies, which means there are plenty of people who like you a lot. Having friends is one of the best signs that a person is beautiful on the inside, not just the outside. So you're a winner already!

Quiz:
✵ Your Beauty Personality ✵

Answer these questions to learn your beauty personality.

1. Whose hair and makeup style do you like best?
   A. Meg Ryan   B. Keri Russell   C. Christina Aguilera

2. Which best describes your hair and makeup routine?
   A. I don't have a routine—I just brush and go.
   B. I do my hair and maybe use a little light makeup.
   C. I do it all! I don't leave the house until I'm all fixed up.

3. What's your ideal outfit?
   A. Jeans and a comfy shirt.
   B. I'm not particular, as long as it's cute.
   C. I'm a glamour girl! Give me fashion any day.

4. How do you rate your beauty knowledge?
   A. I don't pay much attention to that stuff.
   B. I know a few tips and tricks, enough to get by.
   C. I could write a book on beauty! It fascinates me.

5. Which best describes your attitude?
   A. As long as I feel good, I'm happy!
   B. I want to feel good, but I want to look good, too.
   C. If I look great, I don't mind feeling crummy sometimes.

6. How many makeup products do you own?
   A. 0-10   B. 11-20   C. 21 or more

If you answered mostly:

A's You have a no-frills, down-to-earth style. You care about your comfort, and you're not concerned about what other people think.

B's You like to look good, but you're not obsessed with it. You do it because it's fun and it makes you feel good about yourself.

C's You always look fabulous—in fact, you sometimes feel pressured to look great. You believe that beauty is the result of hard work.

Quiz:

❊ What's Your Inner Beauty Factor? ❊

Rate yourself on the following scales. Add up all of the numbers to find your score.

		Neutral				
I like me!	5	4	3	2	1	I wish I were different
I'm thoughtful	5	4	3	2	1	I speak without thinking
I'm an optimist	5	4	3	2	1	I'm a pessimist
I'm friendly	5	4	3	2	1	I think I'm too shy
I'm tolerant	5	4	3	2	1	I sometimes judge people
I care about others	5	4	3	2	1	I care about me
I like to help	5	4	3	2	1	Do it yourself!
I'm responsible	5	4	3	2	1	I let things slide
I like sharing	5	4	3	2	1	All mine!
I'm self-confident	5	4	3	2	1	I lack confidence
I'm mostly happy	5	4	3	2	1	I'm mostly down
I feel inner peace	5	4	3	2	1	I'm often upset
I'm even-tempered	5	4	3	2	1	I get angry easily

If your total is:

52 to 65 There's no doubt about it, you have true inner beauty! No matter what you look like on the outside, everyone loves you because of your kind heart and cheerful nature.

39 to 51 You are well on your way to inner beauty. There are a few areas that are still hard for you, but that's okay. After all, your friends love you just the way you are.

26 to 38 Although you have started on the road to inner beauty, you're not very far along yet. But getting started is the hardest part. If you keep an open mind and an open heart, the rest of your journey will be easy!

13 to 25 You're struggling to find inner beauty. That's okay. Lots of girls go through a difficult phase. Focus on areas that you would like to change and take one small step every day. You'll get there, especially if you let your friends help you.

5

Cool Crafts

Crafts are a great activity at sleepovers, for many reasons. For one thing, it's just fun to make stuff. Every girl loves a cool bracelet she braided herself or a custom toe ring in her favorite bead colors. Another good thing about crafts is that they keep your hands busy, but not your mouth. You and your friends can gossip and giggle all you want as you create your works of art.

But the very best thing about crafts is that they can be taken home as souvenirs. The bracelets, anklets, hair wraps, and other items that you and your buddies make at your sleepover will last long after the party is over, and they will be super reminders of the friendship and fun you all shared!

This chapter includes six neat craft ideas to get you started. You can use them as is, change them to suit your personality, or make up crafts of your own.

Ready? Set? *You go, girl!*

CRAFT BASICS

Here are a few tips to help you organize some can't-miss craft activities for your sleepover.

- **Plan in advance.** You will need special supplies for certain crafts. For instance, you might need colorful floss to make friendship bracelets. You might also want custom beads or other fun materials. Plan your crafts well before your party so you can buy supplies, if necessary.

- **Choose quick crafts.** A sleepover is probably not the time for long or involved projects. Your guests might get bored if an activity takes too long. (Especially if it's late and everyone is a little sleepy!) So pick fairly simple crafts that are easy and fun to do.

- **Keepsake crafts are best.** The best crafts are the ones your guests can take home with them and keep as party souvenirs. (Most of the crafts in this section fit this description.) You could even encourage your guests to swap their creations with one another before leaving your party. That way, the crafts are friendship tokens as well as souvenirs!

- **Get permission.** Get an adult's permission before doing messy projects like pillowcase or T-shirt decorating. It's okay to use things like glue, paint, and glitter in your craft activities, but a grown-up might want to help you set up a spillproof craft area first.

☐ **Gather your materials.** Before the party begins, gather everything you know you're going to need for specific projects. You could also collect a bunch of other craft stuff that you think might be fun. Put it all in a big box in the corner of your party room so you don't have to go looking for it when craft time arrives.

That's it for guidelines. Now let's get creative!

QUICK FRIENDSHIP BRACELETS

This friendship bracelet is about as easy as it gets. It's designed to be quick and fun. If you would like some more challenging patterns, check out your local library or bookstore. There are some good instruction books for friendship bracelets.

Supplies needed:
- Several colors of craft floss
- Ruler
- Scissors
- Tape

Instructions:
1. Cut three strands of floss, each one 3 feet (91 cm) long. (For prettiest results, use three different colors.)
2. Hold the strands so the ends are even. Fold all the strands in half and tie a knot, leaving a small loop above the knot. Tape the loop to a table.

3. Separate the strands by color into three groups, each with two strands. Braid the groups until the bracelet is long enough to go around your wrist.

4. Knot all the strands together at the end of the braided section. Trim the ends, leaving about 3 inches (7.5 cm) loose. Put the ends through the loop to tie your bracelet closed.

JAZZ THEM UP!

You can add beads or charms to your bracelets to make them fancier. You could also make your bracelets thicker by using two or even three strands of each color instead of just one.

FUN FINGER AND TOE RINGS

Now it's time to decorate your fingers and toes with super beaded rings. This craft is so easy and quick that you might want to make rings for everyone you know!

Supplies needed:
- Tiny "seed" beads, assorted colors
- Twist ties
- Scissors

Instructions:
1. Strip the paper or plastic coating off a twist tie, so only the bendable metal wire remains.

2. String seed beads onto the wire. Continue until there are exactly enough beads to go around your finger or toe.

3. Twist the metal wire together to close the ring.
4. Use scissors to trim the wire. Tuck the ends through the beads so you won't get poked when you wear your new jewelry!

BEAR SCARE ANKLET

A "bear scare" is an anklet that you leave on until it gets worn out and falls off by itself. Why is it called a bear scare? Who knows! But one thing is certain: These funky anklets are fun to make and fun to wear, too!

Supplies needed:
- Thin twine or hemp string
- Ruler
- Scissors
- Tape

Optional:
Many stores sell colored string that is about the same thickness as twine. Using two colors of string makes this anklet extra special!

Instructions:
1. Cut two strands of string, each one 5 feet (152 cm) long.
2. Hold the strands so the ends are even. Fold the strands so that two ends are 4 feet (122 cm) long, and two ends are 1 foot (30 cm) long. Tie a small knot at the fold, leaving a loop above the knot. Tape the loop to a table.
3. Arrange the strands so the short ones are in the middle, with one long strand on either side.

4. Knot one long strand around the middle short strands as shown.
5. Knot the other long strand around the middle short strands as shown.
6. Repeat the two knotting steps until the bear scare is long enough to go around your ankle.
7. Put the bear scare around your ankle and tie a knot with all the strands. Trim the ends, leaving about 3 inches (7.5 cm) loose. Put the ends through the loop to tie your bear scare closed. Remember, tie it *tight* so it won't come off!

Step 4

Step 5

SOUVENIR PILLOWCASES

To do this craft, you need a solid-color pillowcase for each guest. (You could use the pillowcases as the goodie bags you hand out at the beginning of the party, if you want.) Then provide all kinds of fabric decorating supplies. Here are some ideas:

- Regular fabric paints
- Puffy fabric paints
- Permanent markers
- Glitter glue
- Sequins
- Sponge stamps
- Stencils
- Iron-on transfers

Let each guest decorate her pillowcase however she likes. The finished pillowcases will be sleepytime souvenirs of your party!

HAIR WRAPS

Hair wraps are pretty and fun. They're not hard to do—but the longer a girl's hair is, the longer they take. You and your friends might want to take turns wrapping if someone's hair is especially long.

Supplies needed:
- Card stock (a file folder is perfect)
- Craft floss
- Tiny rubber bands
- Scissors
- Beads

Instructions:

1. Cut out a square of card stock, then cut a slit in the square. Use the square to separate one thin lock of hair, as shown.

← *Square*

2. Starting at one end of a length of floss, tie a double knot as tight as you can right at the top of the hair strand. Hold the short loose end of the floss along with the hair. Wrap the long end around the hair and the short end. Wrap tightly and close together, so no hair shows.

3. To change floss colors, hold one end of the new floss along with the hair. Wrap over the end with the current color for about 1 inch (2.5 cm). Then trim the old color, leaving about 1 inch (2.5 cm) loose. Hold the end along with the hair and start wrapping with the new color.

4. Continue wrapping until you reach the end of the hair lock. Loop the end of the floss through the last row of wrapping to knot it. Knot the floss and trim the end.

5. Wrap a tiny rubber band around the hair lock right where the floss is tied. This will hold the floss in place.

6. Push a pony bead onto the rubber band. It should be a tight fit so the bead won't fall off.

7. Carefully remove the card stock square.
    Ta-da! You have done a hair wrap!

GRAFFITI WALL

This one is strictly for fun! Get a big roll of brown paper (available at any office supply store). Cover a whole wall in your party room with paper and set plenty of markers and crayons nearby. When your guests arrive, show them the wall and tell them to write or draw whatever they want, whenever they want. By the time the morning arrives, you will have an amazing graffiti wall that reflects the personality of your party!

CHECKLIST: ESSENTIAL CRAFT SUPPLIES

Here's a quick list of everything you need to do the crafts in this section. Check off each item once you have either bought it or found it around your home.

Friendship bracelets:

- Craft floss, three colors ____
- Scissors ____
- Tape ____
- Ruler ____
- Beads ____
- Charms ____

Hair wraps:

- Craft floss ____
- Scissors ____
- Tiny rubber bands ____
- Card stock ____
- Beads ____

Bear scare anklet:

- Twine or hemp string, 2 colors ____
- Scissors ____
- Tape ____
- Ruler ____

Finger and toe rings:

- Twist ties ____
- Seed beads ____
- Scissors ____

Pillowcases:

- One pillowcase for each guest ____
- Fabric paints ____
- Puffy fabric paints ____
- Permanent markers ____
- Glitter glue ____
- Sequins ____
- Sponge stamps ____
- Stencils ____
- Iron-on transfers ____

Graffiti wall:

- Roll of brown paper ____
- Tape ____
- Markers ____
- Crayons ____

List other things you need here.

____

____

6

On-line Fun

The internet is an amazing thing. With an internet connection and a few clicks of the mouse, your home computer becomes the window to a limitless world of information, games, music, beauty, and fun. You can chat with cyber pals, read about your favorite movie and music stars, learn new skills, and much more. Why not bring your sleepover into the cyberspace age and plan some super on-line activities?

There is no way to list every cool web site in this book. There are just too many. Instead, this chapter gives you a few ideas about where to start. You can surf these sites before your party and decide which ones to visit with your guests, or you can check them out during the party as a group.

Before you start, you might want to take the What's Your On-line IQ? quiz on page 74. Using the internet is a blast, but it can be dangerous if you don't follow some basic safety rules. This quiz will test your on-line know-how and ensure that you and your guests "surf safe." Then check out all the Gotta-Know Internet Info on page 75 to make sure you know all the essential internet lingo!

MUSIC MADNESS

The internet is definitely the place to check out the music scene! Surf on over to MTV's web site (**www.mtv.com**) and also to VH1 (**www.vh1.com**) for the general 411 on the music world.

To find specific artists, check out **www.celebrity-fun.com.** This super search engine helps you to find the official web sites of your favorite groups and singers. Here are a few mega-popular addresses to get you started:

Christina Aguilera	**www.christina-a.com**
Backstreet Boys	**www.backstreetboys.com**
Destiny's Child	**www.dc-unplugged.com**
Alicia Keys	**www.aliciakeys.net**
'NSync	**www.nsync.com**
Britney Spears	**www.britneyspears.com**

You can also use the celebrity-fun web site to find the on-line addresses of popular movie and TV stars, TV shows, and current movies. Have fun!

CHAT THE NIGHT AWAY

The internet is absolutely packed with great chatrooms for kids and teens. These are some of the most popular ones:

- www.teenchat.com
- www.teenchatworld.com
- www.preteenchat.com
- www.teen-online.com

You have to create a user name to enter these rooms, so make sure you ask a parent's permission before signing on.

GET GORGEOUS

If you're looking for tips about makeup and other beauty topics, these great web sites will get you going.

- www.covergirl.com
- www.beauty.com
- www.sephora.com
- www.makeup411.com

TEEN TIME

These web sites are designed especially for teens (and they are fun for preteens, too). You'll find advice columns, horoscopes, fashion advice, makeup tips, movie reviews, and more at these addresses. Check them out!

- www.teen.com
- www.ecrush.com
- www.teenfx.com
- www.gURL.com
- www.boycrazy.com
- www.agirlsworld.com
- www.alloy.com

If these sites aren't enough, visit **www.atomic teen.com**. Atomic Teen is a search engine that will help you to find any kind of teen-related site you can imagine.

JUST FOR FUN

Looking for something different to do? All of these sites are awesome. Give them a try.

- **www.amused.com** and **www.bored.com.** Both of these web sites have an assortment of fun and goofy stuff for you to do. You can design your own ice cream sundae on-line, invent polls and e-mail them to your friends, and much, much more.
- **www.limitedtoo.com.** You can create a virtual model that looks just like you, then use your on-line self to try on Limited Too clothing!
- **www.teen.astrology.com.** Horoscope Central for teens.
- **www.americangreetings.com** and **www.blue mountain.com.** Choose from hundreds of animated greeting cards that you can personalize and e-mail to all your friends.
- **www.slingo.com** and **www.pogo.com.** These are cool game sites. Many of these games are for one player only, however. Don't let any of your guests get bored.

www.coolsiteoftheday.com. This web site has enormous lists of the coolest sites on the web. Happy surfing!

Quiz:
❈ What's Your On-line IQ? ❈

Do you know how to keep safe on-line? Take this quiz to find out.

1. If a chat buddy you've never met in person asks for your phone number, what should you do?
   A. Don't forget to include your area code.
   B. Make up a fake phone number.
   C. Just say no!

2. If someone says something offensive to you on-line, you should:
   A. Record his or her screen name, then tell your parents.
   B. Ignore the comment.
   C. Write back and ask the other person to stop.

3. An on-line buddy wants to meet you in person. What do you do?
   A. It's never okay to meet an on-line buddy.
   B. Discuss it with your parents. If they say yes, meet the buddy in a public place with your parents present.
   C. Exchange phone numbers so you can talk to the buddy first and judge whether there is any danger.

4. Someone you don't know has sent you an e-mail with an attachment. You should:
   A. Delete the e-mail without even opening it.
   B. Go ahead and download the attachment. It's probably cool!
   C. Forward the e-mail to all your buddies.

5. You can get a free gift for filling out an on-line survey. What should you do?
   A. Fill it out. The web site probably has good security.
   B. Provide your correct address so the gift will get to you, but put fake information in the rest of the spaces.
   C. Ask your parents for permission first.

6. You accidentally surf onto a web site with pictures you know you aren't supposed to see. You should:
   A. Leave right away and forget about it.
   B. Look around. What your parents don't know won't hurt them.
   C. Leave right away. Later, talk to your parents about what you saw.

Answers: 1C, 2A, 3B, 4A, 5C, 6C

Gotta-Know Internet Info

If you're going to surf the web, you need to speak the language! Here are some common abbreviations and emoticons (symbols that show emotions) you can use, as well as some important netiquette (net etiquette) tips.

Abbreviations:

AKA..................Also known as
ASAP.........As soon as possible
BBL......................Be back later
BFN......................Bye for now
BRB.....................Be right back
BTW.......................By the way
CUL8R................See you later
FAQ..............Frequently asked questions
FYI.........For your information
GMTA.Great minds think alike
HHOK.....Ha ha only kidding!
IMHO.In my humble opinion
LOL..........Laughing out loud; Lots of luck
OIC............................Oh, I see
ROTFL.....Rolling on the floor laughing
SYS.......................See you soon
TTFN..................Ta ta for now
TY...........................Thank you
WB...................Welcome back
YW................You're welcome

Emoticons:

:-) Smiling
:-(Frowning
;-) Winking
:,-(Crying
:-o Uh-oh!
:-O Shocked
:-D Big laugh
:-| Who cares?
:-@ Shouting
~:-(Angry
:-c Very unhappy
:-x My lips are sealed
:-P Sticking tongue out
:-& Tongue tied

Netiquette tips:

- TYPING IN ALL CAPS MEANS YOU'RE SHOUTING. Don't shout when chatting.
- Never use bad language. Many internet providers monitor the behavior of their users, and they might cancel your account if they catch you cursing.
- Use emoticons to make your feelings clear when you're chatting. It's easy for people to misinterpret typed messages.

7

Boys, Boys, Boys!

When you and your girlfriends get together, the conversation probably turns to boys sooner or later. Most girls love to talk about boys, especially which ones they like and which ones might like them back! Cute boys, athletic boys, smart boys, and nice boys are fun to talk about, too. You might even like chatting about the many differences (and similarities— yes, there are some) between boys and girls.

Sleepovers are a perfect time for boy talk because there is absolutely no chance that you will be overheard. (Your parents and your baby brother don't count. They won't go telling your deep, dark boy secrets to the rest of your classmates.) So let it all hang out! Talk louder, longer, and more honestly than you would in school or at the mall. You can just let the conversation flow naturally, or you could give it a little structure with the activities in this chapter. Either way will be fun!

KEEPING IT COOL

Although talking about boys is definitely fun, it can go too far if you're not careful. Here are a few tips for keeping the boy talk under control.

- ☐ **Be nice.** If you're going to talk about people behind their backs, you should say only nice things. Don't let the conversation turn mean-spirited. Think about how a boy would feel if he heard the things you were saying. If something would make him feel bad, then you shouldn't say it.

- ☐ **Be aware of your guests' feelings.** Some girls might be uncomfortable with boy talk, or they might get tired of it after a while. If you sense that a guest is becoming annoyed or bored, it's time to shift the conversation in a different direction.

- ☐ **No teasing.** When you talk about boys, you usually talk about your opinions—who's the cutest, who's the nicest, and so on. You might talk about your feelings, too—who you like the best, who you would like to date, and how you felt when *that guy* talked to you in the school hallway the other day. Opinions and feelings are personal, and the last thing you want is to get teased about them. Your guests don't like it either, so make a "no teasing" rule and stick to it. No exceptions!

- ☐ **Your friends come first.** Don't forget that the whole purpose of a sleepover is to have a good time with your girlfriends. Boy talk can be a fun bonding experience that makes you feel closer to your buddies. But it can also turn the focus of your party away from the friendship that you and your guests share. It's fine to go boy crazy temporarily, but it's your job as the hostess to bring the emphasis of your party back to where it belongs.

By following these simple rules, you will guarantee that the talk stays fun and your guests stay happy!

If just talking about boys isn't enough for you, you might want to organize some activities. Here are a few great guy-related things for you and your guests to do.

YOUR DREAM GUY QUIZ

Everyone can answer the questions on page 80 to learn her dating "type." What is your dream guy like? Find out with this quick and fun quiz!

HOT OR NOT? SURVEY

Make a copy of the survey on page 81 for each girl, including yourself. Let everyone fill out the survey by making a check mark in either the "Hot" or the "Not" space next to each guy's name. Then compile all the answers to see the results.

If you want, you could also revise the "Hot or Not?" survey to include the names of guys at your school.

CHAT APPOINTMENT

Before your party, make a "chat appointment" with a group of boys. Tell your favorite guys that your sleepover group will be on-line and ready to chat at a certain time. When the time arrives, you and your guests can sign on as a group and gab to your hearts' content.

MACHO MOVIE FEST

Rent movies starring actors that you and your friends think are super cute. That way you'll get to enjoy a good movie and watch a hot guy at the same time!

GREATEST GUYS SURVEY

Make up a survey with categories such as "Nicest Guy," "Smartest Guy," "Most Popular Guy," "Most Athletic Guy," "Cutest Guy," and anything else you can think of. Let each girl vote in each category, filling in the names of boys at your school. Tally the votes to see who wins!

Quiz:
✳ Your Dream Guy ✳

Answer these questions to identify your dating "type."

1. What really makes you notice a guy?
   A. A great sense of humor
   B. When he pays special attention to you
   C. His super fashion style
2. Which of these qualities is most important in a guy?
   A. Easy to talk to
   B. Affectionate and considerate
   C. Fabulous looks and lots of friends
3. You would never date a guy who:
   A. Can't carry on a conversation
   B. Doesn't show his true feelings
   C. Isn't part of the "in" crowd
4. Which date sounds best to you?
   A. A fun night at the fair
   B. Walking on the beach and talking for hours
   C. Dinner and a movie—he pays
5. What would be the best gift from a guy?
   A. A coupon for something fun you can do together
   B. A poem he wrote just for you
   C. Beautiful jewelry
6. What should a guy spend his money on?
   A. Whatever makes him truly happy
   B. Surprises that show he's thinking of you
   C. Great clothes so he'll look good when you go out

If you answered mostly:

A's You want a boyfriend to be your best buddy. Your dream guy is easygoing. He'll make you laugh and make sure you have a good time, no matter what you do.

B's You're a romantic! You're looking for that special someone who will never forget to make *you* feel special, too.

C's You're popular, and you want your guy to be popular, too. You know from experience how much work it takes to be "in," and you admire a guy who can play the game.

80

Survey:
❄ Hot or Not? ❄

Are these famous guys and music groups hot . . . or not? You be
the judge! If you don't know a guy or a group, just skip that
line.

	Hot	Not		Hot	Not
Ben Affleck	__	__	Heath Ledger	__	__
Backstreet Boys	__	__	Tobey Maguire	__	__
David Boreanaz	__	__	Ricky Martin	__	__
Leonardo DiCaprio	__	__	'N Sync	__	__
			O-Town	__	__
Aaron Carter	__	__	Ryan Phillippe	__	__
Russell Crowe	__	__	Brad Pitt	__	__
Tom Cruise	__	__	Prince Harry	__	__
Carson Daly	__	__	Prince William	__	__
Matt Damon	__	__	Freddie Prinze, Jr.	__	__
Taye Diggs	__	__	Sisqó	__	__
Eminem	__	__	Will Smith	__	__
Hanson	__	__	Scott Speedman	__	__
Josh Hartnett	__	__	Justin Timberlake	__	__
Josh Jackson	__	__	James Van der Beek	__	__
Chris Klein	__	__			
Ashton Kutcher	__	__	Westlife	__	__
Nick Lachey	__	__			

Write in your own favorites who don't appear on the list:

_____

_____

_____

_____

In the Dark

At some point during your sleepover, the lights will probably get turned off. (It's nighttime, after all.) But just because the room is dark doesn't mean you and your guests will be ready to sleep. If you're like most girls, you will want to keep the party going long after the lights go out!

Luckily, this is easy to do. You can have just as much fun in the dark as you can in the light. In fact, some of the very best sleepover activities, like telling scary stories, absolutely *must* be done in the dark. A sleepover can't be truly fabulous without a few of these classic no-lights activities!

This chapter is full of ideas for things to do in the dark. Some of these games and activities have been around forever. Others might be new to you. Read through the ideas and pick the ones that sound interesting to you, then get ready to crank up the fun factor. Who cares about sleeping? Let's party!

AFTER-DARK ADVICE

All of the tips from the Great Games chapter (see page 31) apply to after-dark games and activities. But there are some additional things you should consider.

- ☐ **Be extra careful.** If you're going to be doing anything active in the dark, you need to be way more careful than usual. Move absolutely *everything* that could hurt you or your friends. (Coffee tables, for example, can bruise shins. Throw rugs can bunch up and trip people.) Do whatever you can to make sure no one gets hurt and nothing gets broken.

- ☐ **Be considerate.** Your parents and other non-partying members of the household may go to bed long before you and your friends are ready to hit the sack. If other people are sleeping, you should play only *quiet* after-dark games. Swapping secrets and telling stories are okay, but rowdy activities like Flashlight Finder (page 85) and Shadow Theater (page 86) probably are not.

- ☐ **Pick your activities carefully.** Some girls love to do scary things like telling "true" ghost stories—the creepier, the better. But spooky stuff scares the daylights out of other girls!

Also, some girls (or their parents) might object to these activities because of their religious beliefs. It is up to you as the hostess to know your guests' preferences and to make sure no one is uncomfortable.

☐ **Honor your word.** You and your parents may have agreed on a firm go-to-sleep time when you laid out the ground rules for your sleep-over. If so, stick to it! If you want to do in-the-dark activities, turn out the lights well before you are supposed to settle down for the night.

That's all there is to know. It's time to turn off the lights, break out the flashlights, and celebrate the night in super sleepover style!

A LITTLE ATMOSPHERE

Sitting around in the pitch dark isn't really that much fun. What you want is *atmosphere*. Try these suggestions to create different kinds of dim—but fun!—lighting.

☐ **Holiday lights**—Hang strings of multicolored holiday sparkle lights around your party room. Turn them on when the overhead lights go off.

☐ **Colored bulbs**—Replace each lamp's white bulb with a colored bulb. (Ask an adult to do this. The white bulbs will be HOT when the lamps are first turned off.)

- **Flashlight fire**—Turn on a bunch of flashlights. Pile them in the middle of the room like logs on a campfire.
- **Starry sky**—Poke holes in a piece of black construction paper, then tape the paper over a flashlight's lighted end. Shine the flashlight upward to create a ceiling of stars!

FLASHLIGHT FINDER

Flashlight Finder is a great in-the-dark version of the game Tag. Here's how it works.

Choose one girl to be "It." That girl sets a turned-off flashlight on the floor in the very middle of the room. The lights are then shut off. (The room should be as dark as you can possibly make it. Close the curtains and stuff towels under the doors to stop any light from entering.)

Once the lights are off, all the girls who aren't "It" scatter to different parts of the room. "It" stays in the middle, a couple of steps away from the flashlight. Her job is to prevent the flashlight from being turned on. Everyone else's job is just the opposite! Girls should try to creep up to the flashlight and turn it on. If "It" tags a creeping girl, that girl is the new "It." But if a girl reaches the flashlight and turns it on without being tagged, then the current "It" must guard the flashlight for another round.

Here's the catch. "It" may not look for hidden

girls. She can only tag them if she hears them heading for the flashlight. So quietness is the key to winning this game!

SHADOW THEATER

If even a few of your friends enjoy acting, then everyone is sure to love this activity. Budding actresses can provide the entertainment. Those who aren't wild about acting get to be the audience, which is just as much fun!

To set up your shadow theater, hang a white sheet across one corner of your party room. (You will probably need to ask an adult to help you.) Leave plenty of space behind the curtain so the actresses will have room to work.

Next, gather a bunch of props—the more, the better. Big stuff like brooms, pans, hockey sticks, and floppy hats work really well for shadow theater. Put all the props behind the sheet where the actresses can get at them easily.

Finally, turn on a few flashlights and put them behind the sheet. Set them near the wall with their beams pointing upward and toward the sheet. There should be a gap between the flashlights and the sheet. That's where the actresses will stand.

That's all you need to do to get ready. To start the main event, turn out the overhead lights and lamps. Send the actresses behind the sheet and tell them to make up the goofiest play they can think of, using lots of props. Spectators will see the scene projected as shadows onto the white sheet. For best results, the actresses should experiment with shadow "special effects" like hiding their arms in their shirts or "sawing" one another in half. From the other side of the sheet, these simple actions look hilarious!

STRIKE A POSE

This activity is simple, but very funny. Choose one girl to be the "poser." Turn off all the lights and give the poser a few seconds to strike a funny pose. Then turn on the flashlight and see what she's doing.

Do this over and over, turning the flashlight off and on and off and on. Each time the flashlight comes on, the poser will be doing a new silly thing that is sure to make everyone laugh! When the poser runs out of ideas, let someone else take a turn.

GUESS WHAT I'M DOING

Turn off all the lights, then have one girl do something that makes noise. It could be something easy, like snapping her fingers or opening and closing a zipper. Or it could be something harder, like brushing her hair or rubbing her hand against the carpet. Anything goes as long as it can be heard.

Now everyone else takes turns guessing what the girl is doing. The first person to guess correctly wins the round. For the next round, it's the winning girl's turn to be the noisemaker.

DRAWING IN THE DARK

Get a bunch of small slips of paper. On each slip, write something that is easy to draw, then drop all the slips into a box.

Here are some things you could put on the slips:

- dog
- monkey
- house
- man
- woman
- baby
- car
- hot-air balloon
- bicycle
- skateboard
- ice cream cone
- guitar
- TV set
- padlock
- hot dog
- beach ball
- umbrella
- sunglasses

Next, get a big pad of paper and some crayons or markers. Give them to one girl. Have her choose a slip from the box and read it to herself. Then turn out the lights while she tries to draw whatever it said on the paper. When she is done, turn the lights back on and see how she did. Can you guess what the picture is supposed to be?

Make sure each girl gets several chances to draw. It's fun!

PALM READING BY FLASHLIGHT

Try a little palm reading! Look at the picture to see the names of some of the lines that appear on most people's palms. Read what each line means.

Then take turns examining one another's palms (use the palm of the person's dominant hand) and making "predictions" about the future.

Remember, this is just for fun. Don't take it too seriously.

All lines should be clean, deep, and unbroken. If a line doesn't fit this description, then you may have a problem in the area indicated by that line. Especially strong lines, on the other hand, show your areas of strength.

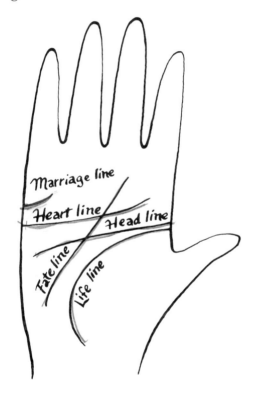

- **Head line**—Reflects your mental abilities. An abnormal head line means stress or other mental problems.
- **Heart line**—Reflects the strength of your heart, both physically and emotionally. An abnormal heart line means difficulties in these areas.
- **Life line**—Reflects your zest for life. An abnormal life line means that your zest is low.
- **Fate line**—The stronger the fate line, the stronger your belief in fate, and the more things fate has in store for you!
- **Marriage line(s)**—Shows a very strong emotional bond to another person. (This bond is not necessarily a marriage, though.) Most people have one to three marriage lines.

SCARY STORIES

Can you imagine telling spooky tales in full daylight? You could do it, but it would be awfully hard to give your friends the creeps—and that's what telling scary stories is all about. Goosebumps, jitters, and shivers up the spine go hand in hand with darkness, so turn off the lights and get ready to get scared!

Let all your guests take turns telling their freakiest stories about ghosts, aliens, monsters, vampires, and other scary stuff. For a spooky effect, the storyteller could hold a flashlight under her chin with the beam pointing upward. The beam highlights some areas of the face and drops others into deep shadow. The result is both strange and scary! Try this while looking in a mirror if you want to see what you look like.

You could also try sitting in front of a dark picture window while you spin your spooky tales. This is creepier than you think. You never know what might come shuffling out of the darkness and . . . AAAAARRRGGGGHHHH !!!

DO-IT-YOURSELF SCARY STUFF

If regular scary stories get boring, you could try making them up as you go along. Have one girl start the story by making up a few sentences. She should stop at an exciting point. Then the next girl continues the story.

Here's an example of how it might work.

Girl 1: I was at my friend Ashley's house one evening doing homework. I was supposed to leave while it was still light, but we ran late. So I ended up walking home in the dark. I was passing a bush when all of a sudden . . .

Girl 2: A giant monster leaped out right in front of me! It had pointy teeth that were dripping spit. "I'm going to eat you," it growled. It opened its mouth wide and leaned toward me. Then . . .

You get the idea. Take turns until your story is complete. You never know how it will turn out until it's done!

The 10 Greatest Things to Talk About in the Dark

1. **Secrets.** Everyone has them. Swap secrets with your friends under the cover of darkness. (Remember, secrets are private! If something is said at your sleepover, it *stays* at your sleepover. If a friend reveals a secret that could harm her in some way, share this information with your parents after the party.)

2. **Dreams.** Have you ever had a really weird dream? Tell your friends about it and let them help you to figure out what it means.

3. **Embarrassing moments.** No one can see you blush in the dark.

4. **Wishes and desires.** What are your deepest, most heartfelt wishes? Share them with your friends.

5. **Fears.** Is there something you are afraid of? Tell your pals. Somehow it's easier to talk about the things that scare you when it's dark.

6. **Goals.** Tell your friends about the things you dream of accomplishing in your life.

7. **Mysteries.** Do you believe in aliens? What about ghosts, the Bermuda Triangle, and Bigfoot? Swap opinions about these creepy mysteries.

8. **Changes.** At this time in your life you are going through a lot of changes, both mental and physical. Comparing notes with your friends will reassure you that these changes are totally normal.

9. **What the future holds.** What will your life be like ten, twenty, thirty, and fifty years from now? Try to predict your future.

10. **The meaning of life.** People have been trying to figure this one out for thousands of years. No one has succeeded yet. But there's a first time for everything. You and your friends might just be the ones!

YOUR FRIENDSHIP STYLE

Every girl has her own friendship style. How do you and your friends match up? Find out by taking this quiz. Do it by flashlight, then talk about your answers. This activity is perfect for the quiet time right before you go to sleep. You can drift off with thoughts of friendship floating through your head!

Quiz:
❊ Your Friendship Style ❊

What kind of friend are you? This quiz will help you find out.

1. The most important thing about friendship is:
    A. Sharing thoughts and feelings
    B. Supporting each other when necessary
    C. Having fun together
2. When you're with friends, you would rather:
    A. Spend time talking
    B. Go shopping
    C. Go to a great party
3. When you're upset, you want your friends to:
    A. Give you advice and comfort you
    B. Just listen if you need it
    C. Back off until you figure things out
4. If two of your friends are fighting, you:
    A. Try to smooth things over
    B. Decide which friend you agree with and take her side
    C. Stay out of it
5. Which best describes your group of friends?
    A. Just a few very close friends
    B. "Serial" buddies—good friends who change every year or two
    C. A big fun gang
6. How would your friends be most likely to describe you?
    A. Caring and dependable
    B. An independent soul
    C. Lots of laughs, tons of fun!

If you answered mostly:

A's Your friends are the most important thing in your life. You give them whatever support they need, and in return you expect them to support you. Your caring personality makes everyone around you feel special.

B's You're self-confident and comfortable with yourself. You love your friends, but you don't lean on them. Other girls admire your independent nature.

C's You love laughing and being in the middle of the action. Life is never boring when you're around, and that makes you popular with guys and girls alike.

Good Morning!

If the morning sun is shining in the sky, then your sleepover is almost over. Pretty soon your friends will say good-bye and head for home. That moment is always kind of sad, especially when everybody has had such a good time.

But don't let yourself feel blue. There's still one big opportunity to have some fun. Morning means breakfast time, and breakfast does *not* have to be boring. In fact, it can be a major party event if you plan it right. So put on your chef's hat and get ready to get cooking once again!

This chapter includes recipes for some incredibly tasty and easy-to-make breakfasts. It also includes important information about wrapping up your party. By using these tips, you will ensure that your guests go home with full stomachs and happy hearts . . . and that they can't wait for your *next* fabulous sleepover!

MORNING DO'S AND DON'TS

The feeling of a sleepover is very different in the morning than in the night. Instead of being pumped up and excited, your guests may be sleepy and cranky, especially if you stayed up super late before going to bed. Here are two important tips for handling the morning crowd.

- **Let people sleep.** Early risers should be considerate of the sleepyheads in the group. Leave the sleep area quietly without waking people up. You should even let girls sleep right through breakfast if they want. If they're too tired to smell the food, they must really need the rest! Just make sure you save them some food so they won't go hungry when they do wake up.

- **Don't worry if the enthusiasm level seems low.** It takes some girls a long time to get going in the morning. Don't push them to show more excitement than they feel. A little down time is good for the soul.

A GREAT BREAKFAST IDEA

Your parents helped you to plan your sleepover. They drove you around town running errands, they paid for supplies, and they probably lost a bunch of sleep during your party. They did all this just to make you happy. Why not return the favor and do something to make *them* happy, too?

Making breakfast for your parents is a wonderful way to say "Thanks for the party!" Pick one of the recipes that follow, or choose something different that you particularly like. Then mastermind the entire meal along with your guests. Prepare the food, set the table, and serve a gourmet breakfast to your parents, the ultimate party hosts. It will be a treat they won't soon forget!

Oh, and one more thing. You and your guests are responsible for tidying up after the meal, too. The great impression you make with your breakfast will be ruined if you make your folks do the cleanup afterward.

Breakfast Banana Splits

Ingredients for each banana split:
- One ripe banana
- One 6-ounce (170 g) container of vanilla yogurt
- 1 cup (.24 l) of corn flakes or bran flakes
- Cool Whip topping
- 1 cup (.24 l) of fresh berries (you can use blueberries, raspberries, chopped strawberries, or any other berries you like)

Who says banana splits are just for dessert? This recipe proves they're not!

To make this delicious breakfast treat, peel a banana. Carefully slit it the long way and lay it in a bowl. Scoop the yogurt onto the banana, then sprinkle the cereal flakes on top. Add a few blobs of Cool Whip, then finish off your breakfast treat by covering it with the fresh berries. It's yummy and good for you, too!

—▬—

Breakfast Burritos

Ingredients for each burrito:
- One egg
- Salt and pepper
- One small flour tortilla
- Grated cheese (Cheddar or Monterey Jack works well)
- Salsa

Break the egg into a microwave-safe bowl. Add a little salt and pepper and scramble the egg. Put the bowl in the microwave and cook the egg on high for 25 seconds. Stir the egg, then cook it for another 25 seconds, or until it is completely done.

Now put the scrambled egg on the flour tortilla. (You might need to break up the egg with a fork first.) Sprinkle grated cheese on the egg, then add a little salsa. Roll up the tortilla and enjoy your tasty breakfast burrito!

—▬—

Fruit Pizza

Ingredients:
- One package of refrigerated sugar cookie dough
- One 8-ounce (227 g) container of cream cheese
- 1 cup (.24 l) of sugar
- One 14.5-ounce (411g) can of mixed fruit

This recipe requires baking. Ask an adult for permission before using the oven. If you're not allowed to use it yourself, you can do all the other parts of the recipe and just have a grown-up help with the baking.

Start the fruit pizza by pressing the cookie dough into a pizza shape on a baking tray. Bake according to the directions on the package. While the dough is baking, mix together the cream cheese and the sugar, then drain and rinse the fruit. Set the rinsed fruit on a paper towel to get rid of extra water.

When the dough has finished baking, remove it from the oven (or have an adult do it for you) and let it cool for about ten minutes. When the "pizza crust" is cool enough to handle, spread the cream cheese mixture on top, then add the fruit. Cut into pizza slices and enjoy!

Simple Cinnamon Toast

Ingredients:
- Slices of bread
- Butter
- Powdered cinnamon
- Sugar

You need to use a toaster and a toaster oven to make this sleepover favorite. Ask an adult for permission.

Making cinnamon toast is super easy. Just toast the bread. Spread plenty of butter on one side. Sprinkle cinnamon and sugar over the butter. Then heat the bread in a toaster oven, butter side up, until the butter bubbles and the sugar starts to melt. Remove and eat!

WINDING THINGS DOWN

After breakfast is over, it's time to start bringing your sleepover to a close. There are a few things you can do to make this process go smoothly.

- ☐ **Ask for help tidying up.** Your guests won't mind helping you pick up the party area. Put craft supplies back where they belong, gather magazines and stack them in a corner, take dirty dishes into the kitchen, and so on. This doesn't have to take long. You're not trying to put things into perfect order; that's your job as the hostess, and you should do it after your guests leave. Right now, you just want to reduce the mess enough for each girl to gather all of her belongings. People will leave things behind if they can't find them.

- ☐ **Allow enough time.** The pick-up time that you wrote on your invitation is the time your guests should be ready to walk out the door. It is *not* the time to start packing! Begin winding down your party early enough to get everything done by the designated time.

- ☐ **Separate everyone's stuff.** Each girl should put her things in a pile, apart from everybody else's belongings. When her ride arrives, everything will be in one place and ready to go—no last-minute scrambles.

THANKS FOR COMING!

As each girl leaves, remember to thank her for coming to your party. You did a lot of work as the hostess, but your party wouldn't have been any fun without your guests. Let each girl know how much you appreciate her participation—*and* her friendship. After all, you can't have a truly fabulous sleepover without truly fabulous friends!

10

Terrific Themes

All sleepovers are great. But if you want to add a little extra sparkle to your event, consider throwing a themed sleepover. It isn't hard to do. Just pick a fun theme, then make sure everything about your party matches that theme. Your invitations, the food you serve, your decorations, your activities, and even the movies you show can all contribute to your sleepover concept.

This chapter includes ideas for a few themed sleepovers. This information isn't meant to be complete. It's really just enough to give you the general idea and get you started. Use the themes in this book or make up your own. Let your imagination run wild. Remember, with a little creativity, absolutely *any* theme can be turned into a fabulous party!

SAFARI THEME SLEEPOVER

A safari sleepover is perfect for girls who love animals and adventure. These ideas will help you to set up a terrific night of jungle fun!

Invitations:

- Make invitations that look like airplane tickets or passports. Let the journey begin!
- Attach each party invitation to a tiny stuffed animal.
- Use animal-print bandannas as invitations. Write the invitation information on each bandanna with brightly colored fabric paint.
- Glue two 5-inch (12.5 cm) cardboard tubes together so they look like binoculars. Punch a hole in each tube and tie a string to the binoculars so they can hang around the neck. Write the party information on a piece of paper, then roll it up and put it inside one of the tubes.

Decorations:

- Put stuffed animals all over the place. The more, the better.
- Get glow-in-the-dark eye stickers (available at party stores). Put them all over the room so you'll see them when the lights go out.
- Hang green and brown streamers from the ceiling to look like vines.
- String white twinkle lights across the ceiling to look like stars.

Food:

☐ Make peanut butter and jelly sandwiches. Then use animal-shaped cookie cutters to stamp out safari sandwiches!

☐ You can also make animal shapes with Jell-O. Follow the instructions on the box to make Jigglers, then use animal-shaped cookie cutters to make lots of fun animal shapes.

☐ Try "ants on a log." To make this fun snack, spread peanut butter all over a peeled banana or a pretzel rod. Coat the "log" with chocolate jimmies. Yuck! It looks like ants!

☐ Set out lots of animal crackers, cheesy goldfish, gummi worms, gummi bears, Teddy Grahams, and other animal-shaped snacks.

Games and activities:

☐ Buy a face-painting kit. At the party, take turns painting one another's faces to look like your favorite animals.

☐ Play animal charades. Write the names of different kinds of animals on slips of paper. Take turns picking a slip, then acting out the animal that appears on the slip. Everyone has to guess which animal the actress is supposed to be.

☐ Arrange a safari scavenger hunt. Hide stuffed animals all over your party room, or even in your backyard if the weather allows. Turn out the lights (or go outside after dark, depending on where you hid the animals) and have everyone try to find all the "wild animals" by flashlight. The girl who finds the most animals wins.

☐ Make bead buddies. Buy bead animal supplies and instructions from a craft store. Let all your guests make as many bead buddies as they like!

Movies:
• *The African Queen*
• *Born Free*
• *Gorillas in the Mist**
• *I Dreamed of Africa**
• *Jumanji*
• *The Lion King*

*Rated PG-13. Ask a parent for permission.

GLAMOUR THEME SLEEPOVER

If dressing up and getting gorgeous is your idea of a good time, then a glamour sleepover is for you! Here are some suggestions for a night of fashion and fun.

Invitations:
☐ Make invitations that look like tickets to a fashion show. Write "Admit One" on each invitation.
☐ Attach each party invitation to a tube of lipstick or a bottle of nail polish.

☐ Write each party invitation on the first page of a tiny notebook. At your party, guests can fill the rest of their notebooks with one another's autographs.

☐ Get a bunch of super-cheap sunglasses to use as invitations. The wilder the sunglasses, the better. Use a paint pen to write the party invitation across the lenses.

Decorations:

☐ A glamorous party is all about stars! Cut out lots of star shapes and hang them all over the room.

☐ Put mirrors everywhere. You and your friends will want to admire yourselves in true fashion-model style.

☐ Provide lots of cheap plastic champagne glasses. No matter what you're drinking, you'll do it with star style!

☐ Hang a sheet or put up a changing screen in one corner of the room. Glamour involves lots of clothes changing.

☐ Set up a special makeup area for each guest. Make a big star with the girl's name on it to identify her area.

Food:

☐ Real models eat lots of low-fat, low-calorie foods to keep themselves slim and trim. Provide carrot and celery sticks, fruit salad, light popcorn, and other good-for-you snacks.

☐ Smoothies are good supermodel food. Just make sure to use healthy ingredients. (For example, you could use nonfat yogurt instead of regular yogurt.)

☐ For drinks, try diet sodas and bottled water. You could also get some sparkling grape juice to drink out of your fancy champagne glasses.

Games and activities:

☐ Take pictures. Fashion models get their pictures taken all the time, and your party should be full of picture-taking, too. Put an inexpensive disposable camera in each guest's goodie bag. Encourage girls to snap away all night long!

☐ Do makeovers. Take a "Before" picture of each girl. Then spend plenty of time helping one another to get as glamorous as possible. When you're done, it's time for the "After" pictures!

☐ Do a photo shoot. Let each girl be the star of her very own photo shoot. The other girls can be photographers. Blast some fun music in the background for authentic photography studio atmosphere!

☐ Arrange a beauty pageant. Each girl gets to compete in three categories: Fancy Dress, Talent, and Q&A. The contestant gets to pick her own fancy dress outfit and talent routine. The judges (the rest of the girls) get to pick the question for the Q&A category!

Movies:
- *Clueless**
- *Drop Dead Gorgeous**
- *Miss Congeniality**
- *Miss Firecracker*
- *She's All That**
- *Smile*

*Rated PG-13. Ask a parent for permission.

MY FAVORITE THINGS SLEEPOVER

There are no specific suggestions for this sleepover. The way it turns out will depend totally on your friends' personalities.

Here's how to do it. On your party invitation, tell your guests to bring some of their favorite things to the party. Be specific! You could suggest things like this:

- Wear your favorite T-shirt, shoes, and earrings
- Before the party, tell me your favorite drink (and then you must provide it)
- Bring your favorite stuffed animal
- Bring your three favorite CDs
- Bring your favorite movie of all time
- Bring your favorite board game

Other "favorites" could include magazines, web site addresses, beauty products, candy, or anything else you can think of. What things will show up at your party? You won't know until your guests start to arrive!

BIRTHDAY HOTEL SLEEPOVER

Of all the suggestions in this book, this one is the most expensive. It also needs to be planned the furthest in advance. But it is great for a really special occasion, like an important birthday. Ask your parents for permission well before the party date, then work with them on the planning.

The first step in arranging a hotel sleepover is choosing a good hotel. The best sleepover hotels have pools, hot tubs, workout rooms, and room service. A room with a kitchenette is especially handy because it gives you more food options. It's also good if the hotel is located near fun stuff like a beach, a mini-golf course, a go-kart track, a mall, or anything else you especially like.

There are a couple of things you do need to ask before deciding on a hotel.

- ☐ **Are there any age limits?** Some hotels do not allow guests under a certain age to use the workout facilities and the hot tub, or to hang out at the pool by themselves. It is possible that your parents might be able to talk to the hotel manager and make special arrangements for your party. But if the rules cannot be bent, then you should pick another hotel.
- ☐ **Ask about the room setup.** The number of guests you can invite to your party will depend on the room. Everyone should have a comfortable place to sleep.

Once you have located your ideal hotel, an adult must make a reservation for you. In fact, the adult will probably need to reserve two rooms—one for the party and one for himself or herself. Don't send out any invitations until the reservations are made! You might not be able to get a room on the day you want.

After the reservations are made, you can create your guest list. Be careful about this. Besides picking the right number of girls, you must also pick the right *type* of girls. You cannot get rowdy in a hotel like you can at home, which means that you and your guests must respect the hotel's rules and behave appropriately at all times. Any girl who might not be able to handle these restrictions should not be invited to your hotel sleepover.

As far as the actual invitations go, they should be handled by your parents, not you. Have your parents call each guest's parents and explain the party to them. Your friends' folks will want to know all the details about time, place, and how the party will be supervised, and they will want to hear it from an adult. So let your parents do the phone duty just this once.

You're almost done! There's just one last thing to do, and that is to set the ground rules for your party. You read about the importance of ground rules earlier in this book. This is even more important when your sleepover will be held away from home. How late can you stay in the pool? Does a parent have to be there? Are you allowed to order room service? Are you allowed to leave the room without permission? All of these things must be discussed, along with anything else that may be important to your parents. Set the rules and then stick to them. Your parents are putting a lot of trust in you and your friends by allowing you to have a hotel sleepover. Show them that you deserve it!